Life in a
Freshwater Lake

Kay Jackson

KIDHAVEN PRESS

An imprint of Thomson Gale, a part of The Thomson Corporation

Detroit • New York • San Francisco • San Diego • New Haven, Conn. • Waterville, Maine • London • Munich

LIBRARY OF CONGRESS CATALOGING-IN-PUBLICATION DATA

Jackson, Kay, 1959-
    Life in a freshwater lake / by Kay Jackson.
        p. cm. — (Ecosystems)
    Includes bibliographical references and index.
    ISBN 0-7377-3145-1 (hard cover : alk. paper)
    1. Lakes—Juvenile literature. 2. Lake ecology—Juvenile literature. I. Title.
II. Series.
    QH98.J33 2005
    577.63—dc22

                                                                    2005014167

Contents

Chapter 1

Freshwater Lakes

A lake is a slow moving or standing body of water surrounded by land. From its sunlit shores to its dark, cold bottom, a lake teems with life. Millions of tiny plants and animals float in its waters. Birds paddle in the thick reeds growing along warm, shallow edges. Frogs plop from floating logs, while raccoons search for insects under rocks. Under a lake's sparkling waves, fish chase insects and sometimes each other in search of their next meal. In a lake's **ecosystem**, water connects everything in a web of life.

Lakes are found all over the Earth. Some lakes are nestled in tall mountain ranges or lie on top of high plateaus. Mapam Yumco Lake in southwestern

Tibet is the highest freshwater lake in the world. It lies at 15,049 feet (4,588m) above sea level near Mount Kailas in the rugged Himalaya mountain system. Hot, dry deserts also hold lakes. Lake Chad, deep in the Sahara Desert of Africa, has water in it year-round. Other desert lakes called playa lakes have water in them only during the rainy season and then dry up for the rest of the year.

Even Antarctica has lakes. Special equipment mounted on space satellites can see through layers of ice. Since 1980 more than 70 lakes have been found beneath Antarctica's thick ice. One lake called

Four herons hunt for food along the shore of a freshwater lake in Louisiana.

Lake Vostok lies beneath 2.5 miles (4km) of solid ice. Deep down, its waters are warm enough to be liquid and not frozen.

The Importance of Lakes

While water covers most of the planet's surface, water that is not salty is hard to find. Only 3 percent of Earth's water is freshwater. Of that small part, an even tinier amount can be used by living things. That is because most of the world's freshwater is frozen in **glaciers** and the polar ice caps or stored deep under the ground. But freshwater lakes have water that living things can use. In fact, 98 percent of usable freshwater is found in the world's lakes.

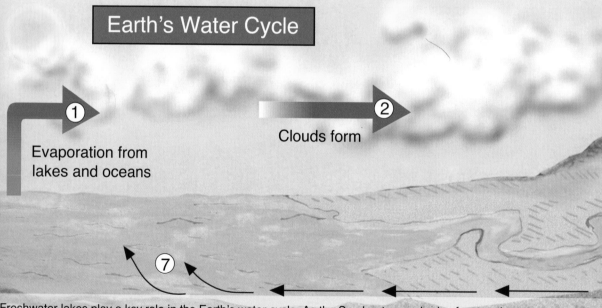

Earth's Water Cycle

1. Evaporation from lakes and oceans

2. Clouds form

7.

Freshwater lakes play a key role in the Earth's water cycle. As the Sun heats up a body of water, the water evaporates into the atmosphere (1), where it forms clouds (2). As the clouds move over the land, they mix with water evaporated from plants and the soil (3). Eventually, water from the clouds falls as

Lakes are an important part of Earth's water cycle. Rain falls to the ground and collects in a stream or a river that then flows into a lake. The sun heats up the lake's water. The water evaporates, or turns into water vapor, and goes into the air. As it rises, the water vapor in the air gets cold, changes back into liquid, and forms clouds. The clouds become heavy with water droplets. Eventually, the water falls back to the Earth as rain, hail, sleet, or snow. The rainwater runs off into a lake, and the water cycle starts all over again.

A lake can be filled in different ways. Some lakes are fed all year long by rivers that flow into them. Others receive water only during the rainy season.

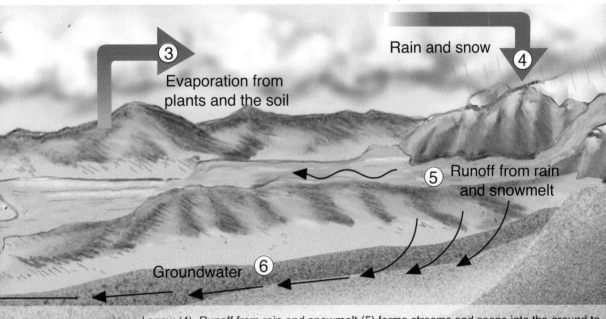

rain and snow (4). Runoff from rain and snowmelt (5) forms streams and seeps into the ground to become groundwater (6). As streams join to become rivers, and groundwater moves through the rocks, the water flows toward lakes and oceans to begin the cycle again (7).

Melting snow and glaciers fill up some lakes. Most lakes, however, are filled with water that comes from below the surface of the land. When rain falls, it soaks into the soil and slowly seeps down into underground layers of rocks. Water flows between the layers of rock. The underground water eventually reaches a lake and helps fill it up.

A Lake Is Formed

In the lands north of the equator, glaciers made most lakes. Glaciers are packed layers of snow that over time turn into sheets of solid ice. Thousands of years ago, Earth's temperatures cooled, and huge glaciers, some more than 1 mile (1.6km) thick, inched down from the Arctic to cover much of North America, Asia, and Europe. Like giant bulldozers, they pushed aside rock, dirt, and boulders. As they scraped along, the glaciers dug deep scars in the land. The Great Lakes of North America and the long, narrow lakes of Norway's coastline were scoured out by creeping glaciers.

Eventually, the weather warmed, and the glaciers melted. As the glaciers melted, they left behind piles of rock, dirt, and sand called **moraines**. The moraines often plugged up the valleys dug out by the glaciers. When these valleys filled with water, they became lakes. The Finger Lakes of New York were made when glacial waters were trapped behind moraine dams.

Glaciers also made kettle lakes. Sometimes, large blocks of ice were stranded as glaciers melted. Like bowling balls stuck in mud, the blocks of ice pressed

Lakes formed when glaciers in the Northern Hemisphere began melting thousands of years ago.

down into the soft dirt. After hundreds of years, the ice finally melted and left behind hollows. Gradually, the bowl-shaped basins filled with water. These basins are called prairie potholes, and they dot the plains from Kansas to the Canadian border.

Other lakes have more unusual beginnings. For example, oxbow lakes were once a part of a river that flowed in wide, S-shaped curves. When the river changed course, the curve was cut off. It became a crescent-shaped lake called an oxbow lake. Other lakes sometimes form in long, deep cracks in Earth's crust called faults. An example of this is Loch Ness in Scotland. This lake is 23 miles (37k) long but only 1 mile (1.6km) wide. It formed about 10,000 years ago when melting glaciers filled a fault with their chilly waters. Lake Chub filled in after a meteorite crashed into Canada. The meteorite's impact made a perfectly round basin. Volcanoes can also create lakes. Crater Lake in Oregon was made about 7,000 years ago when the top of a volcano collapsed and left a crater. Snowmelt and rainwater later filled the hole with water and made a lake.

Lakes that are not made by natural forces are called artificial lakes. These lakes are created by beavers and humans. Beavers stack up branches and logs to make their dams, while human engineers use dirt and concrete. People have been building dams and making lakes for thousands of years. Archaeologists, scientists who study ancient people through the things they left behind, have found evidence of artificial lakes that are 5,000 years old. Some ancient lakes made by people are still used today. For example, Lake Parakrama Samudra in Sri Lanka was built over 1,600 years ago. Farmers still irrigate their crops with its waters.

Life Cycle of a Lake

Many lakes are so large and deep that it is hard to believe they will one day fade away. Lakes, however, do change over time. In fact, a lake begins to change the moment it is formed. Rivers and rainwater carry bits and pieces of rock and sand that settle to the bottom of a lake and start to fill it in. Dead animals and plants also help fill in a lake. Slowly, the lake becomes shallower, and its sandy shores grow toward the center. In the end, trees, bushes, and grasses grow over the land where water once stood. This process can take hundreds or thousands of years.

Usually, it takes a long time for a lake to disappear. Sometimes, though, a severe drought can change a lake filled with sparkling water into a dry bed of blowing

Crater Lake in Oregon was formed when snowmelt and rainwater filled the crater left behind by a collapsed volcano.

This lake in Australia's Kakadu National Park has shrunk dramatically during the dry season.

sand in less than a hundred years. A drought is a long-lasting dry spell that affects a large area of land. During droughts, clouds do not drop their usual amount of rain or snow. Without enough rain, lakes start to shrink.

Each freshwater lake is different. Some are blue and cold, others are green and warm. Old lakes might be surrounded by thick forests while new man-made lakes have shores of gravel and rock. But, no matter what shape, size, or color, each lake is an important part of life on this planet.

Chapter 2

Lake Plants

The ecosystem of a freshwater lake depends on its plants. Plants are the beginning of many of the food chains in a lake, and they provide the oxygen that lake animals breathe. Some plants even keep lakes clean by filtering out poisons. Plants can be found in almost every part of a lake.

Zones in a Lake

A lake is divided into three zones. The zones are based on how far sunlight reaches into the water. Each zone has plants especially adapted to that part of the lake's ecosystem.

The **littoral zone** is closest to the lakeshore. Its waters are warm and shallow. The water depth is about

Lake plants such as these water lilies provide oxygen for animals to breathe.

chest high, and light reaches all the way to the bottom. Most of a lake's plants and animals live in the littoral zone, where there is plenty of sunlight.

Farther away from shore is the **limnetic zone.** The open water of the limnetic zone is often windy and sunny. This zone goes down as far as sunlight reaches. Some lakes are clearer than others, so the limnetic zone may be deeper in these lakes. Tiny floating plants and animals live in this zone.

The **profundal zone** is the deepest one. It is at the bottom of a lake. The profundal zone is cold and dark. No sunlight reaches here, so plants do not grow. Only a few fish and crustaceans, or animals with shells, live in its murky depths.

Everything Depends on Algae

Algae are plantlike organisms found in all but the darkest zones of the lake. Algae are similar to plants, but they do not have true roots, stems, and leaves

The algae growing in this lake produce food for numerous creatures within the ecosystem.

like most plants. Instead, algae have holdfasts and blades. Holdfasts anchor the algae and keep them in place but do not take in nutrients. Algae blades spread out in the water and take in nutrients, but they do not have stems or veins like true leaves.

Producing Food

Algae come in many different shapes and sizes. Some look like tiny dots that can only be seen with a microscope. Others are large. For example, kelp can grow to be 20 feet (6m) long. Some algae grow in long strings that float in a lake like green pieces of spaghetti. One kind of algae looks like fuzzy green hair growing on stumps and rocks.

All life in a lake's ecosystem depends on algae. Algae supply food and oxygen to the other creatures in the lake. They are **producers**, or living things that make their own food. Algae make food through **photosynthesis**. During photosynthesis, algae combine sunlight, water, carbon dioxide gas, and a green substance called chlorophyll to make sugars and oxygen. The sugars are food for algae. Animals breathe in the oxygen made during photosynthesis.

Since algae are primary producers, they are the beginning of many of the food chains in a lake. For example, tiny floating animals called zooplankton eat algae. Small fish, reptiles, and amphibians eat the zooplankton. Larger fish, mammals, and birds hunt these smaller animals. Although algae are important to freshwater lakes, other plants also grow and support these ecosystems.

A Lake's Web of Life

Life on Earth would not survive without the Sun (1). Green plants, such as reeds and algae (2), use sunlight to make sugars. Algae is eaten by tiny aquatic animals called zooplankton (3), and zooplankton are tasty treats for frogs (4). A hungry heron (5) might eat the frog for lunch. When the heron dies, decomposers like snails and bacteria (6) will eat and digest the heron's body. What the decomposers do not eat returns to the water and soil (7) as nutrients. Plants take up the nutrients as additional nourishment, and the cycle begins again.

Stuck in the Mud

Emergent plants grow in the warm waters of a lake's littoral zone. Cattails, reeds, rushes, arrowheads, and wild rice are emergent plants that are found in freshwater lakes. These plants sink their roots in the rich mud along the shore, while their stems and leaves reach above the water to catch the Sun's light.

Emergent plants need sunlight to make food. These plants have different ways of reaching the light at the water's surface. For example, emergent plants like reeds and cattails have long stems that grow as tall as a person. Others like water lilies have round, flat leaves that float like rafts on the water.

Emergent plants play an important role in the ecosystem of a lake. They provide food and shelter for animals that live in shallow water. Small fish hide among their stems, and ducks build nests among reeds far from predators on the shore. Frogs lay egg sacs on their leaves and stems, and newly hatched tadpoles take cover in their shadows.

Large beds of emergent plants such as rushes also help stop **erosion** along a lake's shoreline. When strong waves crash against a lake's shore, the waves wear down its edge by carrying away soil and sand. Erosion can change the gentle slope of a lake's shore to a rocky and steep bank. The tall, thin stems of rushes help protect the shoreline. The soft stems break the force of the waves and slow down erosion.

A trout swims among swaying submergent plants in a shallow lake.

While emergent plants live near a lake's shoreline, another kind of plant grows under the water in the limnetic zone.

Under the Waves

Submergent plants live under the water. Only their flowers reach above the waves. Water currents carry nutrients to submergent plants. These plants take in nutrients and minerals from the surrounding water through their leaves instead of their roots. Leaves with large surface areas help the plants soak up more

A frog pokes its head above a dense mat of free-floating duckweed.

nutrients. The feathery, divided leaves of the milfoil plant, for example, help it take in what it needs to grow. Other submergent plants have wide, flat leaves.

Even though they live under the water, submergent plants still need sunlight for photosynthesis. To reach the sunlight, plants like the bladderwort have small air sacs along their stems that are filled with trapped air. These mini-balloons help the plant's leaves float near the surface of the water.

Free Floaters

The limnetic zone can be too deep for rooted plants. Instead, it has plants such as duckweed that float freely in the water. Duckweed has small, shiny green leaves that are the size of rice grains. It grows very fast during warm weather and can cover the edges of a lake like a bright, green blanket. Insects and other small animals often hide in its dense mats.

Mosses are found in the littoral and limnetic zones. Floating mosses make thick, green mats that bump up against the shores of lakes. Other kinds look like long, silky strands drifting in open water. Even though mosses do not have roots, they sometimes cling to large rocks and branches. Deer and elk eat moss, while snails and small beetles hide in its tiny, green jungle.

Life in the Reeds

In the rugged Andes mountain system of South America between Bolivia and Peru lies Lake Titicaca. It is the world's highest freshwater lake that boats can

A young boy in a reed boat pushes away from the shore of Lake Titicaca in Bolivia.

navigate. Bending in the mountain wind, tall reeds called totora reeds rise above the lake's cold, blue water. These emergent plants are an important part of life along Lake Titicaca.

For hundreds of years, the Uros people of Lake Titicaca have lived among the reeds. They use the reeds to make floating islands by stacking up layers of the reeds. Eventually, these many layers become thick floating platforms. Then, the Uros build their small houses, also made from totora reeds, on the artificial islands. Long ago, the reed islands protected the Uros from attackers.

Somewhere to Hide

Many animals live among totora reeds as well. Ducks and herons hide in the dense tangle of stems. Small reptiles like frogs and snakes live on reed islands safe from the predators that might eat them.

All sorts of plants live in a freshwater lake. Some are so small that a microscope is needed to see them. Others have leaves as long as a person. Lakes are also home to a wide variety of animals that live in and above their waters.

Chapter 3

Lake Animals

While plants are found in the sunny zones of a lake, animals are found in all parts, even the darkest depths. Giant catfish patrol the dark bottom. Snails crawl along the stem of a reed. Clams dig into the lake mud, and spiders skitter on the water's surface. Of all the animals that live in a lake, zooplankton are the tiniest but may be the most important.

Floaters, Skimmers, and Swimmers

Zooplankton are tiny animals that make up the largest group of lake animals. These small animals float about in a lake's open water. Zooplankton have

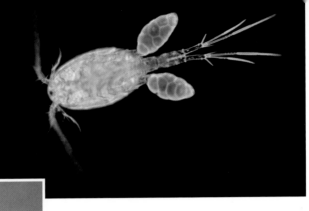

Lakes are home to many tiny animals, including microscopic zooplankton (above) and whirligig beetles (left).

many different shapes and sizes. Some look like torpedoes and have only one eye. Other zooplankton have clear bodies covered in hard shells with short hairs. One kind of zooplankton is so small that hundreds could fit on the tip of a pencil. Others are as long as 2 inches (2.5cm). Zooplankton are **consumers**, or living creatures that eat other living things. They graze on algae and tiny pieces of dead plants and animals.

Lakes are also home to insects. Whirligig beetles skim along the top of the water and dive below it. The beetles take a bubble of oxygen down with them. The trapped air lets the beetles stay underwater for a long time. Newly hatched insects called larvae also grow in lakes. Dragonfly and mayfly larvae swim in a lake's littoral zone. They eat the algae and zooplankton that drift by.

Darters and Snappers

From the pygmy goby, no bigger than a fingernail, to the giant sturgeon as long as a picnic table, many different kinds of fish live in lakes. Silvery shiners dart between rocks near a lake's shore, while colorful perch dash in and out of sunken logs on the lake's bottom. The little fish hide from hungry predators like trout and bass. Bright speckled trout are swift hunters that snap up smaller fish with their powerful jaws. Brown bass with thick bodies are also snappers. They eat fish, frogs, and even snakes.

All fish have special adaptations to living in freshwater. They have gills for removing oxygen from the water. Fish also have air bladders that help them float at a constant depth in the water.

Hoppers and Crawlers

Amphibians and reptiles also live in freshwater lakes. Amphibians are animals that spend part of their lives in water. In many lakes in North America, bullfrogs are heard croaking in the summer. Late in the spring, bullfrog eggs hatch in the warm waters near the shore and quickly grow into tadpoles. The tadpoles spend months in a lake's shallow waters before they grow legs and hop out onto the land.

One of many amphibians living in lakes, a green frog makes a meal of a dragonfly.

Freshwater turtles have flatter shells than land turtles and webbing between their toes. These adaptations help the turtles swim easily through the water. Because turtles are cold-blooded animals, they often crawl onto logs or rocks during the afternoon to soak up the sun's warmth. While freshwater turtles spend much of their time in the water, they build their nests and lay their eggs on land.

Hunters, Paddlers, and Waders

Freshwater lakes also provide birds with shelter, food, and water. For birds that migrate, or travel long distances, lakes are important stops along their way. Birds also build nests and raise their young near lakes. Because lakes provide shelter and food, many different kinds of birds live near lakes.

High above a lake, brown eagles and blue king-fishers hunt small animals like mice, snakes, and fish. They soar, dip, and dive as they search for food. When a hunter sees a tasty meal, it swoops down and snatches up its prey with strong talons.

Instead of flying high over a lake, paddlers like ducks, geese, and swans spend much of their time near a lake's shore. These birds stay out in the shallow water and away from the claws of hungry hunters. Paddlers often build their nests in beds of reeds. Their eggs are safely hidden among the stems and leaves.

Whooper swans jostle for position as night approaches on Kussharo Lake in Japan.

Unlike paddlers, wading birds walk along the edges of a lake. Little sandpipers skitter up and down a lake's sandy shores. In a lake's shallow waters, ibises poke their long beaks into the mud. They search for insects and other animals that crawl along the bottom of a lake.

While lakes provide birds with food, shelter, and water, birds also give back to a lake's ecosystem. Some eat fruit from trees and shrubs. Birds cannot digest the fruit's seeds and pass the seeds in their droppings. This helps to spread the seeds around the lake.

Diggers, Builders, and Grazers

In addition to birds, fish, reptiles, and amphibians, lakes are home to many mammals. Mammals are warm-blooded animals with fur or hair. Raccoons dig in the mud for clams or turn over rocks as they look for crayfish. Families of beavers build dams on lakes in North America. Deep in the dam is the family's den. The den keeps them warm in the winter and safe from hunters like wolves and cougars.

Grazing animals also wander the edges of lakes. In the cold northern parts of North America, Asia, and Europe, giant grazers like elk and moose nibble on water plants that grow in the shallow waters. In warmer places, enormous hippopotamuses feed on plants in the warm waters of African lakes.

An elk makes its way through shallow lake water in search of water plants to graze on.

Mammals have an important role in the freshwater lake ecosystem. Mammals are consumers. Consumers eat plants and other animals and help to maintain a lake's balance. For example, elk and moose can eat huge amounts of water plants every day. Without these grazers, mosses and water plants might grow too quickly and choke out other plants along the shores of a lake.

This crayfish lives among the rocks on the bottom of a lake, where it feeds on bits of dead animals and plants.

On the Bottom

Other living creatures live on the cold, dark bottom of the lake far from the sunny shores. On the bottom, crayfish, or crustaceans with hard outer shells, scuttle from rock to rock. They eat small bits of dead plants and animals that drift down like falling snow.

Clams and other mollusks burrow in the mud of a lake's bottom. Mollusks have hard shells that protect their soft insides. Mollusks also have special gills, or membranes, that filter out oxygen and nutrients from the water.

On the bottom of a lake are **decomposers**. Decomposers are at the end of a lake's food chain. They help organic material to rot. When animals or plants die and sink to the bottom, microscopic creatures called bacteria break down the organic material. The rotting material returns as nutrients in the lake's water and soil. The nutrients help plants and animals to grow.

Fish Found Worldwide

Cyprinids are one of the world's most common types of fish, and they benefit from the work of the decomposers. They live in lakes in Europe, Asia, Africa, and the Americas. Many cyprinids are small and are often called minnows. Some, however, grow to be very big. The mahseer, a cyprinid of India and Southeast Asia, can grow to be 6 feet (1.8m) long. Cyprinids include carp, shiners, and chubs.

Cyprinids are different from other fish. They do not have scales on their heads or teeth in their jaws. Instead, they grind up their food using teeth in their necks. Cyprinids also do not have a stomach. Instead, they have a big intestine.

Cyprinids are important to humans. In many parts of the world, people grow carp for food. People also use cyprinids as pets. They are popular aquarium fish and include tetras, zebras, barbs, loaches, and goldfish.

Cyprinids, like this goldfish, are common in lakes worldwide.

Many plants and animals depend on the world's lakes. Humans also need freshwater lakes. To protect freshwater lake ecosystems, the needs of people have to be balanced against the needs of nature.

Chapter 4

People and Lakes

For thousands of years, freshwater lakes have given people food to eat, water to drink, and a place to live and play. People often built their homes, farms, and towns near lakes. The promise of plenty of clean water still draws people to the shores of freshwater lakes. But, as more people crowd around the world's lakes, freshwater ecosystems have changed.

Water to Survive

Every day, people all over the world rely on freshwater lakes. Cities and towns depend on lakes to supply homes and businesses with water. Lake water is pumped to city water plants, where the water is cleaned. People use the clean water for drinking, cooking, and bathing. Lake water is used in other ways, too.

Farmers use lake water to irrigate their crops. In fact, almost 30 percent of the world's surface freshwater is used to water crops. Irrigation lets farmers plant large fields that grow enough food for all the people in the world.

Factories use lake water to make many goods and products like paper, clothes, computer parts, and cars. Almost every manufactured, or factory-made, product uses water during some part of the

A team of rowers propel themselves across Lake Union in Seattle, Washington.

production process. While lake water helps to make things that meet people's basic needs, it also provides recreation.

Each year, millions of people go to freshwater lakes to enjoy their natural beauty. Children and families splash in their warm waters. Fishers cast lines with baited hooks and hope for a big catch. Bird-watchers stand quietly with binoculars, waiting to catch a glimpse of their favorite bird. As people use lakes more, new lakes are made to meet their demands.

Artificial Lakes

For thousands of years, people have blocked rivers with dams to create artificial lakes called **reservoirs**. During long dry seasons when rain did not fall, rivers and lakes often dried up and water became scarce. To solve this problem, people built dams to make reservoirs that could store water. These artificial lakes were like enormous storage containers. They were often the main source of water during long droughts. Just like in ancient times, dams and reservoirs are still important.

Today, huge dams hold back enormous amounts of water. In the United States, one of the world's tallest concrete dams, called the Hoover Dam, holds back the waters of the Colorado River. Lake Mead spreads out for miles behind the dam. Lake Volta in Ghana on the west coast of Africa is the world's largest man-made lake. When China completes the Three Gorges Dam across the Yangtze

When completed, China's Three Gorges Dam on the Yangtze River will create one of the largest reservoirs in the world.

River, it will be larger than the Hoover Dam. Also, its lake will cover more area than Lake Volta.

Over the last hundred years, large cities have come to rely on water from reservoirs. Desert cities especially need the water from these artificial lakes. For example, Phoenix, Arizona, lies in the middle of the Sonoran Desert. Usually, less than 8 inches (20cm) of rain falls each year in this dry land. Yet 3.5 million people live in and around Phoenix, and thousands more move in each year. The desert's natural lakes and rivers do not have enough water for all of these people. So a chain of four reservoirs was built along the Salt River north of Phoenix. Without these reservoirs, Phoenix would not have enough water to keep growing.

While dams and their artificial lakes are important, the lands flooded by new reservoirs often wipe out important ecosystems. For example, in the 1960s, Glen Canyon Dam was built across the Colorado River. Its reservoir, Lake Powell, flooded miles of desert canyons and their ecosystems.

Another problem is that dams sometimes ruin places that are important to humans. The building

Three Chinese farm boys stand in a cornfield flooded by the rising waters of the Three Gorges Reservoir.

of the Three Gorges Dam has forced more than 1 million Chinese villagers and farmers to move, and many ancient temples will be flooded when the dam is finished.

Human Demands

Over the centuries, the human need for water has changed many freshwater lakes. Some of these changes have been harmful. In fact, some lakes have almost disappeared. People have taken out more water than rainfall can put back in. Lake Chad in Africa is an example of a vanishing lake. For decades, there has been a drought in the deep Sahara. As less rain fell each year, people had to take more water from Lake Chad to use for farming and drinking. The lake is now only 5 percent of the size it was 30 years ago.

Lake ecosystems are also harmed by overfishing when people remove too many fish. Lake Malawi, Africa's third largest lake, shows what happens when a lake is overfished. For generations, fishers of Malawi were able to catch enough fish to feed their families. But when the population of Malawi doubled over the last 50 years, the fishers soon were removing fish faster than new ones could hatch and grow up. As a result, many different kinds of fish have disappeared from the lake.

Lake Pollution

Pollution also changes lakes. Towns and cities sometimes dump sewage from toilets directly into lakes. Factories pump poisonous chemicals into the water. Farmers use chemical poisons called insecticides and pesticides, which are carried by irrigation water into lakes. Fertilizers that are put on crops to make them grow better can flow into lakes. Manure, droppings from farm animals, sometimes also washes into rivers, streams, and lakes.

Over time, a polluted lake can die. The chemicals and poisons kill the fish and plants in the lake. If animals like birds or raccoons eat the poisoned fish, they can become sick. The animals that depended on the lake plants and fish starve or move away. Even though there are polluted lakes around the world, people can clean them up.

Protecting Lakes

Lake Erie is an example of how people can help fix the harm they have done. Lake Erie is one of North America's Great Lakes. By the 1960s, Lake Erie was very polluted. Its oily brown waters smelled bad. Dead fish washed ashore, and people were afraid to eat anything caught in it. Some even called it a dead lake.

Then in the 1980s, the people of Canada and the United States decided to bring Lake Erie back to life. The two countries passed laws to stop factories and cities from polluting the lake. Volunteer groups picked up trash on its shores. It took twenty years, but Lake Erie is once again a living lake. Though the cleanup is not finished, people and fish now enjoy the clean waters of Lake Erie.

Industrial pollution from factories along Lake Michigan can harm its ecosystem.

There are many ways to protect the world's freshwater lakes. Government leaders can pass and enforce laws against releasing dangerous chemicals, garbage, and sewage into lakes. Groups and organizations like school clubs can volunteer to pick up trash along the shores of a local lake. Another simple way to protect lakes is to use less water. For example, families could take showers instead of

Volunteers for the Audubon Society pick up trash alongside a lake in San Diego, California.

baths. Or people could turn off the water when they brush their teeth. Cities could plant trees that need little water to grow.

From the tiny green algae that float near the bright surface to the enormous catfish that lurk on the dark bottom, all sorts of creatures thrive in the world's freshwater lakes. Even though they seem to be indestructible, lakes need the care and respect of people who use them.

Glossary

algae: Plantlike organisms that grow in sunlit waters. Algae do not have true roots, stems, and leaves like most plants.

consumers: Living creatures that eat other living things.

decomposers: Organisms like bacteria and fungi that break down dead plants and animals.

ecosystem: An environment in which plants and animals live together.

emergent: Describes plants that grow in the warm waters of a lake's littoral zone.

erosion: The wearing away of a landform such as a mountain, hill, riverbank, or lakeshore by wind, water, or ice.

glaciers: Enormous sheets of solid, moving ice made from packed layers of snow.

limnetic zone: Far away from shore, the open waters of a lake to the depth where sunlight penetrates.

littoral zone: The area in a lake closest to the shore.

moraines: Piles of rock, dirt, and sand left behind as glaciers retreat.

photosynthesis: The process in plants and algae of combining sunlight, water, carbon dioxide gas, and a green substance called chlorophyll to make sugars and oxygen.

producers: Living things that make their own food.

profundal zone: The region at the bottom of a lake where no sunlight reaches.

reservoirs: Artificial lakes created when a dam is built on a river to store water for drinking and other human uses.

submergent: Describes plants that live under the water.

For Further Exploration

Books

Sandra Donovan, *Animals of Rivers, Lakes, and Ponds*. New York: Steadwell, 2002. This book explains the physical characteristics, behavior, and life cycle of the great blue heron, giant water bug, raccoon, and snapping turtle.

Randy Frahm, *Lakes: Timeless Reservoirs*. Mankato, MN: Creative Education, 2003. Describes how lakes are formed, the plants and animals that live in lakes, and how people use lakes.

Rebecca L. Johnson and Phyllis V. Saroff, *A Journey into a Lake*. Minneapolis, MN: Carolrhoda, 2004. Provides general facts about freshwater lakes, including details about the plants and animals that live in or around a lake.

Melissa Stewart, *Life in a Lake*. Minneapolis, MN: Lerner, 2003. This book shows how the plants and animals that live in Lake Superior depend on each other.

Web Sites

Kids Do Ecology (www.nceas.ucsb.edu/nceas web/ kids). This site introduces world biomes, gives a

43

summary of freshwater ecosystems, describes the plants and animals that live in freshwater ecosystems, and explains the interaction between people and freshwater biomes.

The Water Cycle (http://ga.water.usgs.gov/edu/watercycle.htm). Published by the U.S. Geological Survey, this site explains the water system and shows how it is important to the health of the planet.

What's It Like Where You Live? (http://mbgnet.mobot.org). Sponsored by the Missouri Botanical Gardens, this site allows students to explore life in land biomes and aquatic ecosystems, including freshwater lakes and ponds.

The World's Biomes (www.ucmp.berkeley.edu/glossary/gloss5/biome/index.html). Created by the University of California's Museum of Paleontology, this site describes five major biomes and the importance of each. Includes aquatic, grassland, desert, forest, and tundra biomes.

Index

Picture Credits

About the Author

Kay Jackson writes nonfiction books for children and educational material for teachers. She has written books and articles about the theory of plate tectonics, the world's landforms, King Tut, forest fires, ants, and tarantulas. She lives in Tulsa, Oklahoma, with her husband, daughter, son, one brown dog, and two striped cats.